H. E. Cohen

Ways and Means

The financial Statement of the Honorable H. E. Cohen

H. E. Cohen

Ways and Means
The financial Statement of the Honorable H. E. Cohen

ISBN/EAN: 9783337151317

Printed in Europe, USA, Canada, Australia, Japan

Cover: Foto ©ninafisch / pixelio.de

More available books at **www.hansebooks.com**

WAYS AND MEANS.

THE

FINANCIAL STATEMENT

OF

THE HONORABLE H. E. COHEN,

COLONIAL TREASURER

OF

NEW SOUTH WALES.

MADE 31st JANUARY,

1878.

SYDNEY : THOMAS RICHARDS, GOVERNMENT PRINTER.

1878.

FINANCIAL STATEMENT.

Mr. Garrett,

I beg to move that "There be granted to Her
Majesty, out of the Consolidated Revenue Fund, the
sum of £1,733, to meet expenses in connection with
the Establishment of His Excellency the Governor
for the year 1878." In submitting to the Committee
this item as the formal initiation of the Financial
Statement, I have to appeal to Honorable Members
for the indulgent exercise of their forbearance whilst
I discharge the arduous, and to me novel, task in
which I am now engaged,—an indulgence I the more
earnestly and perhaps justifiably claim by reason
of the very limited period permitted to me for pre-
paration, in view of the necessity of proceeding as
early as possible with the business of the Session,
and the desirability in the interest of the Country of
obtaining as speedily as practicable the necessary
Supplies for the year 1878, which, in the normal
condition of things, would have been granted by
Parliament anterior to the close of 1877.

The system which has obtained during the past three years, of periodically making temporary provision for the Public Service by monthly Supply Bills, is one which stands emphatically condemned upon Constitutional grounds, and also by reason of the serious delay and inconvenience which follow in the prosecution of Public Works, the votes for which are not finally appropriated by Parliament until late in the year for which the expenditure is authorized. The present Administration deeming it to be one of their paramount duties to provide the proper remedy for this unsatisfactory state of things, have decided upon asking Parliament to grant the necessary Supplies for the year with all convenient speed. Considering the overflowing Exchequer, which has of late years released the Finance Minister for the time being from all-anxiety as to the sufficiency of his resources to meet the requirements of the Country, and which now substantially exists in the shape of "Special Deposits" and advances to "Loan Acts," it might be assumed that there existed no difficulty in guiding or managing the financial affairs of the State; but the rational desire of all right-thinking persons, imbued with an anxiety to see our annual income "proper" co-extensive with our annual expenditure "proper," and the equal desire, not to say solicitude, of any Colonial Treasurer alive to his official responsibility to equalize the revenue and expenditure "proper," still impose upon him the duty and care of fully providing the

Ways and Means required for the year with which he is dealing, irrespective of any moneys accumulated from previous years and available for the necessities of the State, and I trust I shall before resuming my seat satisfy the Committee that I have not failed in this respect. I claim no indulgence or freedom from criticism for views which do not commend themselves to the approval of Honorable Members—though I venture to hope that mine will not be unacceptable to the Committee—but I simply ask for indulgence personal to myself in consideration of the limited experience I am able to apply to the important duty in which I am now engaged.

It is not my intention to elaborate or burden my speech with voluminous statistical comparisons to demonstrate the progress of the Country; that, for the time-being, is best and sufficiently indicated in a general way by the large annual returns now being made to the public coffers, and, *inter alia,* in a more specific mode by the substantial increase in our Customs Revenue, in the earnings of our Railways and Telegraphs, and in the receipts from the Post Office,—these establishments being amongst the most important parts of our national revenue-providing machinery, relying for support upon the improved social condition of the people and the general expansion and development of our large commercial, agricultural, pastoral, and mining interests. Statistics I can understand being used as a basis and proof of Budget calculations, but for any other purpose they appear to me to be scarcely apposite to a Financial Statement in Committee of Ways and Means.

With these prefatory observations I shall now apply myself more immediately to an exposition of the financial accounts of the Country, and may here conveniently remark that when hereafter using the unqualified term " Revenue," I wish it to be understood as meaning the entirety of our income or receipts, of whatever nature they may be, as distinct from the narrower designation, " Revenue Proper;" and further, that to a large extent, in mentioning amounts, I shall for convenience sake state them in round numbers as they appear in the Accounts, since the exact figures will be seen by those Accounts and by the Explanatory Statement which will be placed in the hands of Honorable Members during the evening.

It will no doubt be in the recollection of Honorable Members, that the Administration which, on the 22nd December, 1876, through its then Colonial Treasurer, the Honorable Member for East Sydney, Mr. Stuart, laid upon the Table of the House the Estimates for 1877, retired from power in March of the following year, before those Estimates had been considered, and that the succeeding Government, of which the late Honorable Member for the Hawkesbury, Mr. Piddington, was Finance Minister, found it expedient to submit fresh Estimates for the approval of Parliament. In consequence of that and other changes of Government during last year, additional Estimates were brought forward, both then and at a later period, which resulted in so materially altering the public accounts as to render it desirable, nay necessary, that an explanation of these alterations should be given, with the view of conveying a clear and definite understanding of their present position.

The Hon. Member, Mr. Stuart, who made his Financial Statement on the 24th January, 1877, estimated that the Revenue of that year would amount to £4,908,410, the Expenditure to £4,181,952, and the accumulated Surplus at the end of the year to £2,406,066. Mr. Piddington, who made his Statement on the 2nd May, and had therefore the actual Revenue of four months to guide him, estimated the Revenue at £5,308,410, or £400,000 in excess of Mr. Stuart's, the Expenditure at £4,843,937 (inclusive of re-votes of 1876 to the amount of £415,924), and the accumulated Surplus at the close of the year at £2,524,059. Subsequently, Mr. Piddington submitted two Additional Estimates for 1877, amounting together to £2,626,395, which included £2,023,550 for Railway Works, such as had on previous occasions been provided for by Loans. This large additional expenditure would have more than absorbed the Surplus, but for the circumstance that at the time it was submitted the Revenue was largely exceeding the estimate of May, which, taken in connection with the probability of there being large savings on the

8

appropriations of 1877, would still have left a considerable credit balance.

The Government which came into power in August last, of which the Honorable Member for Parramatta, Mr. Long, was Treasurer, withdrew that portion of the Additional Estimates of their predecessors which had not been dealt with by the Assembly in Committee of Supply, and submitted others from which were omitted all the items included in Mr. Piddington's for the construction of Railways, which were however embodied in a separate Loan Estimate. By this arrangement the estimated Surplus at the close of 1877 was not interfered with to any great extent.

From the Ways and Means, which I will submit at a later period of the evening, it will be seen that the actual Revenue of 1877 amounts to £5,751,879, and the Expenditure, which is still, to a certain extent, only an estimate, to £5,530,056, and the estimated accumulated Surplus on 31st December last to £2,317,343.

The Revenue of last year has therefore exceeded Mr. Stuart's estimate by £813,469, and Mr. Piddington's by £443,469.

The Accounts which will be submitted in elucidation of the present and prospective condition of the Consolidated Revenue Fund are of the usual character, viz.:—

An Account of Revenue and Expenditure for 1876.

An Account of Revenue and Expenditure for 1877.

An Account of Estimated Revenue and Expenditure for 1878.

With respect to the Account for 1876, very little explanation is necessary, as the result now shown differs from that previously given to the extent of only £36,735. In the Ways and Means submitted in May last the accumulated Surplus was estimated at £2,059,586. In consequence of certain changes which took place last year, but mainly from the lapsing of additional appropriations, the Surplus for that year is now estimated at £2,096,321. Full particulars of all the changes in this account will be found in the Explanatory Statement which I will at the close of my speech lay upon the Table for the information of Honorable Members.

Coming now to the Account of Revenue and Expenditure for 1877, I have to point out that the one now submitted differs essentially from that submitted by Mr. Piddington in May last; then it was necessarily an entirely estimated Account; now it shows more definitely the actual results of the year's operations, especially so far as the Revenue is concerned.

The Revenue, which was at that time estimated to yield £5,308,410, actually reached £5,751,879, that is £443,469 in excess of the estimate. Taking now the actual result of each year, it will be seen that the Revenue of 1877 exceeded that of 1876 by the very large sum of £714,217; and while there can be no doubt that the larger part of this increase has arisen from the sale of Crown Lands, a very fair and gratifying proportion has been derived from other sources, which indicate in a more marked and, I think, in a more satisfactory degree, the general advancement of the Colony and the continued even flow of that tide of prosperity which first made its presence known through the finances of the Country in 1872.

Comparing a little more in detail the Revenue of 1877 with that of 1876, it may be interesting to note the more salient items of increase, and for a few moments to give our attention to them. First, then, we have "Customs" with £62,861 increase, the total receipts from this source being £1,011,872 in 1876, as against £1,074,733 for 1877. This outcome for 1877, apart from the monetary benefit which has accrued to the public exchequer, tells with undeniable cogency that our commerce, or, in other terms, the consuming power of the population, is increasing, which in its turn signifies the greater aggregate ability of the people to spend, even in face of a succession of seasons which have been of late of the most trying character to all our great interests.

Under this special branch of Revenue, Spirits show an increase as between 1876 and 1877 in favour of the latter year of £34,000 ; Tobacco and Cigars, an increase of £19,500; Sugar and Molasses, an increase of £7,000; Dried Fruits, an increase of nearly £8,500; and specific duties, an increase of nearly £28,000. These results must on the whole be very assuring to the Country; for whether such additions to our Revenue, springing as some of them do, from what has been termed "Voluntary taxation," arise from the more ample means of individual consumers, or additions to our population, or from both causes, they bear testimony to the steady growth of our community, and its power to provide itself with many of the luxuries of life.

"Licenses" show an advance of £7,373, to which "Retail Fermented and Spirituous Liquor Licenses" contribute £6,300. The receipts of the years I am comparing as they stand in chronological order, being respectively £80,302 and £86,602. Whether this in itself is a proof of true and substantial progress upon which the Country may be congratulated is a question upon which opinions may differ; but the figures as they are "will point a moral and adorn a tale," according to the proclivities of the individual mind that may study them.

The "Sales of Land" for 1877 have overleapt those for 1876 by £427,128, having realized for the later period £2,841,203, the particulars of which are given in the "Detailed Revenue," attached to the "Ways and Means," which will be distributed amongst Honorable Members. The great and apparently irrepressible desire to purchase Crown Lands by auction which prevailed at the commencement of the year has since given unmistakeable signs of having been brought under restraint; and, apart from other extra-Governmental causes that have produced this downward tendency in this branch of income, the present Administration has determined to place some restriction upon the alienation of our waste lands by this particular method.

"Interest upon Conditional Purchases" for 1877 shows an advance upon 1876 of £27,325, having attained a total of £126,654, as against an estimate of £130,000, an approximation of figures which speaks favourably of the calculations made upon available official data by the officers to whom this duty is entrusted. Bearing in mind that a year of unusual severity, by reason of the absence of rain, has been experienced by the class of persons by whom this sum has been paid, it testifies strongly to their readiness to liquidate their public liabilities when we find them meeting this claim of the State with so much promptitude and completeness.

"Railways," to which I shall hereafter refer more fully, have returned for 1877 £121,500 above the earnings of 1876. This is a fact which must commend itself with a welcome to every colonist, interested as each one is in the success of this the greatest of all our national undertakings.

The " Post Office," which includes the Telegraph Department, has during 1877 yielded £33,567 over and above the yield of 1876, and to this I need only direct the attention of the Committee as evidence of the growth and onward march of our young Country.

" Bank Deposits" have, in 1877, for interest, given us £31,773 more than in 1876; but as I purpose dealing hereafter somewhat more amply with this feature in our finances, I shall now pass from it with this bare reference.

Having thus briefly alluded to some of the main features of last year's Revenue, I will now as briefly direct the attention of the Committee to its Expenditure.

As originally estimated by Mr. Piddington, the Expenditure of 1877 amounted to £4,843,937, which included appropriations of 1876 for Public Works to the amount of £415,924, which had to be revoted as charges against the year 1877. Subsequently, Further Additional Estimates were submitted by Mr. Piddington, only a small part of which was voted prior to the change of Administration that took place in August last. On the re-assembling of Parliament after that change the Additional Estimates then before the Assembly were withdrawn, excepting such as had been dealt with in Committee of Supply, and others substituted for them. These changes resulted in appropriations by Parliament for General Services, under the Act

41 Vic. No. 8, to the amount of ...	£4,696,249
To which have to be added the appropriations under Constitutional and Colonial Acts	47,947
Special Appropriations	837,000
Further Special Appropriations, as shown in the account now under review	159,253

Making a total authorized charge of ...	£5,740,449
To this there has also to be added the amount of the Supplementary Estimates now before the House, viz. :—	100,407

Which brings the charge against the year 1877 up to	£5,840,856
As on former occasions, however, there must be deducted from this sum the amount of appropriations not likely to be required, which are estimated at	310,000

thereby reducing the estimated expenditure to	£5,530,856
Deducting this Expenditure from £5,751,878, the Revenue of last year, there is left a surplus of ...	221,021
Which, added to the Surplus brought from 1876, viz.	2,096,322

produces an estimated accumulated Surplus on the 31st December last of	£2,317,343

which is less than that estimated by the late Hon. Member for the Hawkesbury (Mr. Piddington) by the sum of £206,716, a difference which will be found more fully accounted for in the Explanatory Statement already referred to.

It will be seen on reference to the Explanatory Statement that the years 1872 to 1877, both inclusive, have each yielded a portion of the Surplus which at the close of 1877 amounted in the aggregrate to £2,317,343.

The Surpluses of 1875 and 1876 necessarily differ to a considerable extent from those previously given, because since then the estimated expenditure of the former year has been reduced by further lapsed appropriations, and the latter by the transfer to 1877, under the head of " Re-votes," of a large amount of appropriations for Public Works, which could not be carried out in the year for which they were provided.

As the Expenditure of these six years; that is from 1872 to 1877, includes a number of payments of an extraordinary nature, it is only right to state them as they occurred, so as to give a clearer idea of the extent of the Revenue over the ordinary Expenditure of the Country. Thus, in 1872, we paid off Treasury Bills and Debentures to the amount of £409,900 ; in 1873. Debentures to the amount of £20,500 ; in 1874, Treasury Bills and Debentures to the extent of £357,100, and payments were also made under the Superannuation Act Repeal Act to the amount of £98,403, making together for that year £455,503. Then, in 1875, Debentures, part of the Public Debt, were paid off to the extent of £74,700; in 1876 further payments of a like nature were made to the extent of £760,200, and during 1877 to the amount of £33,200, besides a transfer under Parliamentary appropriation of £175,838 from Revenue to Loan Fund, 36 Vic. No. 17, to make good the amount short-raised under that Act. These payments, which aggregate £1,929,842, of course form part of the excess Revenue of these years, as much as the Surpluses shown above do. In other words, that sum is part of the Surplus devoted to special Services, with the sanction of Parliament.

During the period over which this large Surplus has accumulated, the amounts realized by the sale of Crown Lands have increased from a comparatively small sum to one that is now considered out of all proportion to the ordinary income of the Country. Excepting in 1872, when the ordinary Revenue was slightly in excess of the ordinary Expenditure, the Land Sales have unquestionably been the source from which the Surpluses have sprung. The tabulated figures in page 8 of the Explanatory Statement of the Public Account will prove this, but they are so

17

voluminous that I will not now weary the patience of Honorable Members by reading them.

Before passing to the Account for 1878, for which I am more immediately responsible, and in which I am naturally more interested, I desire to furnish the Committee with some information regarding the state of the Public Accounts generally, on December 31st last, as exhibited by the books of the Treasury. On that date the Balances to the credit of the various Public Accounts of the Government stood thus :—

Public Account—

Consolidated Revenue Fund	... ...	£2,351,074
Old Loans Account	...	178,915
Trust Fund	... ...	1,006,425
		3,536,414
Special Loan Funds	... ...	530,975
Superannuation Repeal Fund	...	3,758
In all	...	£4,071,147

This amount, which exceeds the aggregate Balances of 31st December, 1876, by the sum of

B

£562,081 18s. 4s., was distributed in the following manner, viz. :— Bank of New South Wales—

London Branch—
Balance as shown by Statement made up to 31st August, 1877 ... ...£16,125
Remittances since that date...750,000

766,125

Head Office, Sydney—
Public Account 394,677
Special Loan Funds ... 409,733

804,410

Total in Bank of New South Wales ———— £1,570,535

Special Deposits in the undermentioned Banks, in accordance with the Banking arrangements of May, 1876, viz. :—

Bank of New South Wales ...	£350,000
City Bank	250,000
Oriental Bank	250,000
Australian Joint Stock Bank ...	200,000
Bank of Australasia	175,000
English, Scottish, and Australian Chartered Bank ...	175,000
Union Bank	175,000
London Chartered Bank ...	175,000
Mercantile Bank ...	175,000

1,925,000

Total Cash Balance £3,495,535
To which have to be added Securities in the Treasury Chest to the amount of 575,612

Making a Total as above shown of ... £4,071,147

Having now finished with the Accounts down to the close of 1877, I will ask the attention of the Committee to the Estimates of the present year. The estimated Surplus brought forward from 31st December last, and appearing on the Credit side of the Account for 1878, is £2,317,343, and I estimate the Revenue for this year at £4,873,750. These two sums together make £7,191,094. Deducting from this the estimated Expenditure for the year, namely £4,723,689, there is left an estimated Surplus at the end of 1878 of £2,467,405. It will, however, be observed that the Revenue as estimated for the year is £150,000 more than the estimated Expenditure. The Expenditure is made up of charges for general Services, £3,879,506, which is exclusive of the vote of £30,000 for the Treasurer's Advance Account,—a sum that does not ultimately form a charge on the Consolidated Revenue Fund; special appropriations, £797,000; and sums provided by Constitution and Colonial Acts, £47,133.

It will, I am sure, not be required of me to point out each item in the proposed expenditure upon which substantial increases or decreases have taken place as compared with last year. The Estimates placed in the hands of Honorable Members will at once give this information; but I may perhaps be pardoned for trespassing upon the time of the Committee in referring more specifically to the vote for Immigration and one or two others.

In the Estimates of Expenditure the Government have included £75,000 for the purposes, of Immigration,—a sum which they deem sufficient, considering that a small portion of the year will have elapsed before it can be legally available for disbursement, and that it is about the amount actually expended for 1877. We are of opinion that a judicious and continued stream of immigration is highly desirable in the interests of the Colony; each individual added to our population representing a consumer and taxpayer, and in many cases a producer also. It is not our object or desire to bring labour to the Colony to compete with that already here, but the experience of the past year or two affords abundant evidence that a steady flow of judiciously selected labour may be imperceptibly and advantageously absorbed into and blended with our population. It has been the care of the Government to inform themselves of the trades which are full-handed, and to instruct the Agent General by telegraph not to assist members of such trades to emigrate.

My Colleagues, as well as myself, are impressed with the folly of bringing to these shores any class of persons who it is obvious could not, without the greatest difficulty, if at all, find occupation upon arrival; but at the same time we feel convinced that there is ample room and opportunity within our boundaries for the employment and advancement of numbers of willing and industrious people, who by thrift and perseverance may make homes and competences for themselves and kindred, and contribute to the making of a happy and thriving nation. We feel confident therefore that the Committee being informed that all previous votes have been exhausted will cheerfully grant the sum now asked for this special Service.

With regard to Public Instruction, for which provision is sought to the extent of £320,000, being £40,000 in excess of the sum appropriated for 1877, I am sure it needs no effort from me to recommend the proposal to the unanimous approval of Parliament. All persons seem agreed upon making adequate, nay liberal, provision for this important feature in our internal polity; and I am certain therefore that this Assembly will, like its predecessors, willingly accord a generous support to the Public School system, and give its cordial approval to our proposal.

In view of the general and long sustained demand, almost universally acquiesced in, for legislation to provide (amongst other things) for increased endowments to Municipalities, and an increased revenue for the Corporation of the City of Sydney, and the probability of no such measure passing into our Statute Book before the year is well advanced, the Government have decided to make provision for temporary assistance as well to all Municipalities in the country as to the Corporation of the metropolis, and will therefore ask the House to grant

10s. for every pound received by the former for rates during the municipal year ending the 4th February, 1878, and by the latter during the year ending 31st December, 1877. The sum required for this purpose is estimated at £56,500.

With these special references to items of expenditure I shall now take up the estimated Revenue for the year, which is £4,873,750, being less than the actual Revenue of 1877 by £878,129, the difference being substantially accounted for by our making the estimated receipts for 1878 from auction sales nearly a million pounds less than the actual receipts for 1877. As already intimated by my honorable colleague, the Premier, the Government have determined to take up the question of amending the Land Laws, and after having laid their proposed Bill upon the Table this Session, to deal with it during the next, and therefore, in considering the financial position and prospects of the Country for the present year, I take the law as it exists. We calculate that Auction Sales will realize £1,000,000, which includes £250,000 of balances due on auction purchases made in 1877; improved purchases, &c., £200,000; selections after auction, £160,000; deposits on conditional purchases, £425,000; instalment on conditional purchases, £10,000; balances on conditional purchases, £60,000; thus aggregating for the year under Land Sales £1,855,000.

It will thus be seen that the sum calculated to be realized in the present year from auction sales is

£1,000,000, of which £250,000 represents balances
due on auction purchases made in the last quarter of
1877, leaving £750,000 to be raised from actual
sales during 1878. But as it is the purpose of the
Government not to fix a uniform upset price of £1
per acre upon land disposed of by auction, but to
raise the price according to the quality of the land
put up and the demand for it, this £750,000 does not
necessarily represent 750,000 acres; for as the
average upset price increases, the total area sold to
yield a given sum will decrease in corresponding
ratio; thus, if the average price be 30s. an acre,
the area disposed of to produce £750,000 will be
500,000 acres, and if 40s., the area will be 375,000
acres. In thus managing the auction sales the
object of the Government will be to get for the
State the full value of the land parted with, and to
prevent it passing in wholesale quantities into the
hands of single purchasers, without an accompanying settlement corresponding to the acreage and
nature of the land alienated.

Under "Annual Land Revenue" we anticipate
receiving for interest upon Land Conditionally
Purchased, £155,000; for Pastoral Occupation,
£237,450; for Mining Occupation, £13,000; for
Miscellaneous Land Receipts, £28,500; making a
total of £433,950.

Honorable Members will observe that the amount
of interest on Land Conditionally Purchased calculated to be received this year is £155,000, being

little more than £28,000 in excess of the actual revenue from this source last year. I would here point out that it is practically impossible to make an exact calculation of the interest that will be paid in any given year, in consequence of the number of conditional purchases that lapse or are from time to time forfeited or cancelled or upon which the balances may be paid; it can at best be but an approximation based upon departmental data, but I have every reason to believe that the estimate will be realized.

The yield from "Customs" this year, inclusive of the "Murray River Customs," is estimated at £1,094,700, or £20,000 beyond the actual receipts for 1877. Honorable Members will observe that I have calculated the "Murray River Customs" Revenue at £80,000, as against £82,000 received last year and £120,000 received in 1876. This large difference between the actual receipts for 1876 and 1877, which has guided me in fixing my estimate for the current year, and on the surface would indicate a considerable decrease in our Murray River or South and South-western Border trade, calls for explanation, which will show that it is the result merely of the diverting of the collections from one point of our Colony to another. In order to make this perfectly clear it must be remembered that the Bonds which have hitherto been regarded by the Customs' Department as the " Murray River " Bonds are those at Moama,

Albury, Corowa, Wentworth, Euston, Swan Hill, Tocumwall, and Howlong; and the receipts from these, added to the commutation paid by South Australia under the Convention with New South Wales, have been classed as "Murray River Customs" receipts. During the years 1876 and 1877 the collections from these different places have been as follows :—

		£	s.	d.		£	s.	d.	
Moama	in 1876	54,012	5	11	as against	23,198	16	5	in 1877
Albury	,,	32,740	5	7	,,	31,650	13	7	,,
Corowa	,,	11,556	13	7	,,	10,225	18	9	,,
Wentworth	,,	13,017	15	11	,,	5,112	7	3	,,
Euston	,,	1,145	19	4	,,	1,091	4	5	,,
Swan Hill	,,	480	17	5	,,	491	13	1	,,
Tocumwall	,,	1,336	8	0	,,	638	9	1	,,
Howlong	,,	1,364	10	2	,,	1,143	13	2	,,
South Australia (cash payments).	,,	4,406	11	4	,,	8,489	11	2	,,
Total	...	£120,061	7	3		82,042	6	11	

This shows a falling off in 1877 as compared with 1876, at Moama of £31,000, and at Wentworth of £8,000, these being the only places to which by reason of the great decrease in receipts I need refer, although there have been slight decreases at all the other Bonds except Swan Hill, where there was a nominal increase. Towards the latter end of 1876 —the year, it will be seen, in which Murray River Customs gave us £120,000—Bonds were established at Deniliquin, Hay, and Wilcannia, which not being classified as Murray River Bonds, the collections at these places have been included in the general and not in the Murray River Customs' receipts.

Deniliquin, for four months of 1876 that the Bond was opened, gave us £4,642; Wilcannia, for four and a half months, £1,833; and Hay, for one month, £391. But coming to 1877, we find that these Bonds contributed to the Revenue £24,319, £5,667, and £7,573 respectively, making a total of £37,559.

With respect to the cash payments just shown to have been made by South Australia in 1876 and 1877, it is essential to observe that they were made direct to us by the Government of that Colony, and represent a portion only of the whole sum payable by that to this Government, under the Conventions in existence in those years. Under these Conventions, all duties collected on importations from South Australia by New South Wales, at the bonded warehouses on the Murray or its tributaries coming within the Treaties, were to be accounted for by New South Wales, or in other words, were to be regarded as payments on account of the Treaty commutation. It is the difference between such collections and the total sum payable by South Australia under agreement, which is represented (wholly or partly, as the case may be) by these cash payments. These collections, which embrace the amounts received at the Wentworth, Wilcannia, Hay, and Bourke Bonds, being those covered by the Convention, though credited to South Australia in our account with her, have been treated in the Treasury books as ordinary Customs receipts. The £4,406 paid in 1876 represents the whole difference between the collections by New South Wales on behalf of South Australia and the entire sum payable under the Convention by South Australia to New South Wales for the 1876 Treaty year. The £8,489 paid in 1877 is only portion of the difference for that year, there having been a balance of over £11,000 due by South Australia on 31st December last, under the Convention for 1877.

Seeing then the geographical positions of the townships to which I have thus pointedly drawn attention, and connecting them with the concurrent decreases and increases of duty collections just detailed, it is patent that there has been no actual decrease in the amount of the Murray River Customs generally, but that the collections have merely drifted from some of the old to other and more convenient points. For the purpose of demonstrating more succinctly the conclusion at which I have thus arrived, I will state the figures in form of account :—

In 1876 the Customs Collections at the Murray River
Bonds as defined were £120,061

Add to this—

The amount collected at Deniliquin (4
 months) £4,642
  " Hay (1 month) ... 392
  " Wilcannia (4½ months) 1,833
       together ——— 6,867

 thus making a Total of £126,928

In 1877 the Customs Collections at Murray River
Bonds as defined were ... £82,012

Add to this—

The amount collected at Deniliquin	...	£24,319		
„	„	Hay ...	...	7,573
„	„	Wilcannia	...	5,667
		together...		37,559

Thereby bringing the amount up to ... £119,601

And if we add to this latter sum the £11,367 (portion of which has since been paid) due by South Australia on the 31st December last under the Convention, we will have £130,969 for 1877, as against £126,928 for 1876. I hope I have now made it apparent, at least so far as this collation of figures can do so, that our trade in the direction referred to has not declined. The result of this explanation is to prove that the general Customs Receipts for the year have been increased by the collections at certain Inland Bonds at the cost of reducing the Murray River Customs receipts under the old classification of stations, without the trade connected with the one in any degree affecting the trade connected with the other.

Having in the course of my investigation into this matter discovered that some confusion in the accounts had arisen since the establishment of additional Bonds in the interior, I have issued such instructions as will I think show in future the Customs collections in a clearer and more intelligible shape. I have deemed it my duty to enter thus lengthily into an examination of this subject, because of the general interest which has been manifested regarding it.

Our income from "Receipts for services rendered" is estimated at £1,203,400, as against £1,119,359 for 1877; and on reference to the Ways and Means it will be seen that the receipts from Railways are estimated at £875,000, being £75,000 in excess of the sum actually received for 1877, which in turn was £55,000 more than the estimated receipts for that year.

At the close of 1877 we had open for traffic 597½ miles of Railway, which cost £8,850,000, the net earnings being approximately calculated at £402,900, or £4 11s. per cent. upon the capital invested; but as there were several extensions opened when the year was more or less advanced, on one of which traffic was carried for two months only, we may conclude that had there been a full year's net earnings of these extensions to set off against their cost, which is included in the £8,850,000, the net return upon the entire expenditure would have been somewhat larger.

There are now under construction the following lines :—Orange to Wellington, 85 miles; Cootamundra to Wagga Wagga, 51½ miles; through Wagga Wagga, 4½ miles; Wagga Wagga to Albury, 77 miles; Quirindi to Tamworth, 38 miles; Weriss Creek to Gunnedah, 41 miles; making in all 297 miles ; and we anticipate that the extension from Quirindi to Tamworth will be completed in August next, and that from Cootamundra to Wagga Wagga in September next. The extension of Railways into the interior, resulting as it does in a corresponding growth in their earnings, must be highly gratifying.

Considering the destructive drought which for some time past has been asserting itself with serious effect upon those great interests of the Colony to which the Railway must look for support, we have in the large actual return for 1877 an all-sufficient demonstration of the greatness of the inherent resources of the Country, and their wonderful elasticity and power of expansion, as well as an ample warrant for expecting the full realization of our estimate of Railway Revenue for the current year.

The opening of the line to the south as far as Cootamundra has already had the effect of bringing to Sydney a large number of wool clips which had not previously found their way thither, and of making this the buying market for customers whose purchases had been previously made elsewhere. In these facts we have further foundation for the long-entertained belief that the nearer we approach the Southern boundary of our Colony, the greater will be our carrying and general trade in that direction, and the sooner will we witness the fulfilment of the prediction that, by the construction of the line to Albury (for which my honorable colleague the

Minister for Works has recently accepted tenders), we will secure for ourselves the greater part of the large and important trade of Riverina, which has been heretofore enjoyed by Victoria. The completion of the line to the west as far as Orange has had a most beneficial effect in developing the trade in that direction and in giving producers in that rich and fertile district a market for their produce in Sydney, of which they could not previously, so easily, or to so great an extent, if at all, avail themselves.

Apart from the broad national policy which calls for the opening up of the interior by the construction of Railways, we have the fullest encouragement given to us to proceed rapidly with their extension, in the knowledge that already they are producing a net return almost equal to the percentage of interest payable on the loans raised for their construction. This, in a community of about 650,000 persons, scattered over an extensive area of country, is a result of the most gratifying character.

In this young Colony the rapid extension of Railways is of great importance; primarily because they promote settlement upon the lands of the interior, and give an impetus to the efforts of the producer, who is brought thereby into speedy and easy communication with the great central market of the metropolis and the other markets of the large towns of the interior; and secondly, because, as it fortunately happens, they are a great revenue-producing machinery, producing revenue in perhaps that most acceptable of all forms, compensation for valuable and important services rendered, the benefit of which is not limited to the individual for whom they are directly performed, but is spread indirectly and unseen far and wide throughout the length and breadth of the land; and thirdly, because they impart a higher value to that splendid territorial heritage of which we are the temporary guardians.

I may here, in passing, express my regret, which is I am sure only the echo of the general feeling both within and without the walls of this Chamber, that the Great Northern Line, which is now yielding a net return of $5\frac{1}{2}$ per cent. upon the capital invested in it, should not have reached beyond Quirindi, one extension only of 25 miles having been opened during the past six years; but I may venture to assure the Committee that under the administration of my honorable friend and colleague, the Member for Paddington, a little more vigour will be infused into the operations of the contractor, and that the whistle of the iron horse will ere long be heard in Tamworth. The recent changes made by the present Government in the management of our Railway system, which is assuming such enormous proportions, will, it is hoped and we ourselves believe, have the effect of remedying many if not all of the grievances in connection with the traffic which have of late been so much and so loudly complained of.

From " General Miscellaneous Receipts" we expect to derive £128,700, but from this grouping there disappear this year " Tolls and Ferries," which last year produced £18,552. This is consequent upon the resolution of the late Assembly abolishing all Tolls on Roads, Bridges, and Ferries. I have also excluded from the Estimates of Revenue the item of Stamp Duty, as it is too problematical whether any, and if so what, payments will be made to warrant me in inserting any amount in the Estimates of Ways and Means. It does not follow from this omission that the Government is renouncing any of its rights in respect of arrears of Stamp Duty ; all that is done is simply to abstain from taking them into account in making our financial calculations for the year, pending the Government obtaining the necessary authority to enforce such payments as were due when the Stamp Act lapsed.

Having now specially dilated as fully as I purpose upon the Estimated Revenue for 1878, I shall recur once more to the proceeds of " Land Sales" by auction or otherwise (which are not Revenue strictly speaking, but the State capital converted from its original form), and to the Expenditure these proceeds should provide for; and for the purpose of determining what are "Proceeds of Land Sales," I will adopt substantially the test and sub-

c

division of my honorable friend the Member for East Sydney, Mr. Stuart, viz. :—

1. Sales for cash, in which the operation is at once completed.

2. Sales for a cash deposit, with limited or unlimited credit for the remainder, but subject to the annual payment of interest, whether alone, as under the Land Act of 1861, or amalgamated with the principal, as under the Lands Acts Amendment Act of 1875.

Various opinions exist as to what expenditure is fairly chargeable against the proceeds of Land Sales as above defined. I think that any expenditure upon any permanent public work, whether or not reproductive, upon any work which tends to improve or render more valuable the public estate, and encourages and facilitates the introduction and settlement of population upon it, is fairly chargeable against them. The employment of portion of the capital in these ways enhances the value of the capital remaining, so that whilst upon the one hand we may be diminishing the "quantum" of that capital, on the other, so long as the intrinsic value of the lessened quantity remains equal to if not greater than the original larger quantity, no loss can be sustained.

It is the population of a country that makes it great, prosperous, and wealthy, for without population there would be no produce obtained from the land—the origin of all wealth; there would be no local consumers, and no enterprise to give value to that produce, even when yielded, by introducing it into foreign countries and creating and stimulating an external demand for it; in effect, the land would be comparatively if not absolutely valueless. But with that population in existence, every facility should be afforded to reach the markets for the produce it may raise; and to achieve this object, expenditure in the construction and repair of our public highways, whether these be the ordinary roads or the railways, or the bridges necessary to make them traversable, may, in my opinion, be legitimately made from this source.

I further think that money expended upon our other permanent Public works and upon our Public buildings (which are too voluminous in character to be detailed), upon Immigration, and upon Public Instruction, at least so far as the Parliamentary vote includes the cost of sites and school buildings, may be justifiably taken from this fund. Over and above these, a large proportion of the departmental expense of the Lands Offices being rendered indispensable in consequence of the largely increased staff required to manage and administer the national estate by reason of these sales is, in my opinion, properly provided for from their proceeds. Any items which would not come strictly within the principles I have thus laid down, but which have been usually made the subject of Loan Votes, it will be readily conceded, may also be chargeable against these proceeds ; and that the Public debt may be paid off with them I do not think any person will venture to dispute.

There is no necessity for me to enter upon a justification of the past expenditure of this special income ; that has already been done with more or less completeness by Ministers who have preceded me, but I deem it my duty not to avoid showing specifically how I propose justifying the absorption of such portion of the estimated proceeds of Land Sales for the current year as may be required for the Services of the year :

The estimated Expenditure for the general Services of the year is £4,723,689

The estimated Revenue exclusive of Land Sales 3,018,750

Thus leaving to be provided for by proceeds of Land Sales £1,704,939

Against which I think I can fairly and justly set off the following items included in the General Services :—

1. Public Works and Buildings, excluding £33,950 for annual repairs £221,192
2. Roads and Bridges 512,771
3. Miscellaneous Railway Construction and Building Services ... 125,000
4. Construction of Telegraphs ... 58,800

5. Harbours and Rivers Improvements	£ 98,408
6. Immigration	75,000
7. Public Instruction—purchase of Sites and erection of School Buildings	125,000
8. Departmental expenses of Lands Office (in part)	255,000
9. Endowments and assistance to Municipalities	86,500
10. Aid of Buildings of Schools of Art, and Hospitals, and Agricultural Societies	22,000
11. Portion of the Million Railway Loan of 1866 to be paid off this year	27,000
12. Refund of Land Revenue ...	100,000

Which together make a Total of £1,707,671

An amount embracing items which I trust the Committee will agree with me in considering fair and legitimate charges against the proceeds of Land Sales; but over and above this absorption of so much of the Land Fund there will remain an estimated surplus of £150,000.

But apart from our own economic views as to the proper or improper application of this special branch of our income, it may not be uninteresting to inquire what the public creditor who is deeply concerned in the management of our affairs thinks of our administration in this regard. I think it may be reasonably presumed that they in England, who have lent money to the extent of millions of pounds to this distant part of the Empire, make themselves acquainted with its internal condition and management, or, at any rate, take care to inform themselves of its sources of revenue or income, out of which either the annual interest upon, or the corpus of the national liability is to be defrayed. If this be so—and it is by no means a violent presumption—I think we may flatter ourselves, considering the high price of our Debentures in London, that the English investors, whose great central market is the crucial test of a nation's credit, entertain little if any doubt of the soundness of our administration, or of the wisdom of the course we have been pursuing in alienating our lands and applying the proceeds of their sale as we have done.

Leaving now this feature in our finances, I would take up another to which, much attention has been and is still naturally directed, viz., the large surplus which, representing sales of land, has accumulated during the past four or five years, and which at the end of December last was estimated to amount to £2,317,343. The possession of so large a surplus at the credit of the Consolidated Revenue Fund, and unappropriated by but at the command of Parliament, I regard, under the circumstances of the Colony, as neither an unmixed good nor an unmixed evil; for it is prone to produce a laxity in the control of the public expenditure, and tends to weaken that rigid economy which is exercised by a wise governing body in voting supplies, when all the ways and means necessary to cover them are derived from revenue cotemporaneously raised. Let us see however if any and what beneficial use has been made of the public moneys which from time to time were not required for the current needs of Government.

It will be remembered that my honorable friend the Member for East Sydney, Mr. Stuart, when Minister of Finance and Trade, deeming it desirable to terminate the then existing arrangements for the conduct of the public Banking business, entered into negotiations with the Bank of New South Wales for the future management of the Public account, and subsequently, in May, 1876, submitted to Parliament his draft proposals, which, after amendment by the Assembly, were accepted by the Bank as the basis of its relations with the Government of this Colony.

By that agreement, which was entered into for three years (but is terminable upon notice by the Bank, or after resolution by the Assembly, and notice by the Treasurer, therein stipulated for), the Government is empowered and authorized to place any portion of the public moneys, when the balance to the credit of the "General Banking Account" exceeds £350,000, on special deposit with the Bank of New South Wales and other Banks in Sydney, at a rate of interest not exceeding 4 per cent. per

annum; and acting upon this authority, my predecessors have made special deposits with nine of the
Banks, including the Bank of New South Wales, to
the aggregate amount of £1,925,000; but in addition
to this we received under that agreement interest
at the rate of 3 per cent. upon the daily credit
balance of the " General Banking Account " in
excess of the sum of £50,000, which is free from
interest.

The interest accrued under our Banking arrangements during the years 1873 to 1877 is as follows :—

1873	...	... ...	£11,432
1874	...	... ...	25,613
1875	...	... ...	38,269
1876	...	... ...	52,629
1877	...	... ...	89,130

Making a total of ... £217,073
which I admit has not been altogether derived from
our accumulated Surplus, as the public moneys deposited with the Banks included Trust and Loan
Funds. This amount of interest having been applied
towards meeting the annual expenditure of those
years, assisted the taxpayers of the Country to that
extent to meet the current expenses of Government;
and this use of it I consider perfectly justifiable and
defensible, it being a recurring annual profit made
out of that fund which, in part, represents the capital
of the Country, and in no sense or in the slightest
degree does it affect or reduce that capital.

Passing temporarily from that governmental action which affirmatively assisted the people of the Country to meet the public demands, let us inquire what course was taken to utilize these moneys and avoid the imposition of further liability upon the people. The late Member for Newcastle, Mr. Lloyd, when at the Treasury, initiated the wise practice in 1873—continued by his successors as opportunity offered—of making advances from the Consolidated Revenue Surplus, on account of the different funds established by the Loan Acts passed since then, authorizing the borrowing of moneys for the prosecution of the various Public Works therein provided for. It must be patent to every one with the slightest knowledge of these matters that, in seeking a loan in the great money markets of the world, it would be necessary, as well for the national credit as for securing the most advantageous terms, that the loan should be floated in large amounts, and necessarily at a comparatively long period prior to that when the money would be actually required for disbursement. It would certainly have been impossible to have advantageously procured these moneys by loan in such small sums or at such opportune times as those when the whole of these various advances took place, and hence it is clear that a large saving has been effected by these operations.

But to place something more definite before the Committee, let us compare what the position of the Colony would have been, as regards the interest upon Loans, in the absence of this Surplus, and the position she has been in with it.

It is obvious that in the former case we would have been compelled to borrow at least the £1,600,000 advanced to the Loan Acts; and by a statement which I have had prepared, showing these various advances, with interest at 4 per cent. per annum calculated upon them from their respective dates down to December 31st, 1877, I find that the interest amounts to £94,895, and that is the sum which the Country would have had to pay in the shape of interest had the moneys been borrowed at a like rate on the days when and in the amounts in which these advances were severally made. But being in possession of the Surplus, the Country has not had to pay this £94,895. If, therefore, we add this sum to the £217,073 of actually earned interest already alluded to, we have a total definite money gain to the State of £311,968, which, however, would have been subject to reduction to the extent of any small increment of interest arising out of the temporary banking of borrowed moneys under the present Bank agreement, since that increment might have been applied to part payment of the interest due on those moneys, and thus have reduced "*pro tanto*" the amount of interest to be provided for from other sources.   •

Let us proceed now to other considerations showing advantages springing out of our "*embarras de richesses.*" We cannot forget and pass by as trivial the beneficial effect upon our credit in the great investing markets produced by our abstention from borrowing whilst still carrying on our great Public Works; indeed this is practically shown by the unprecedentedly high prices our securities command in the Mother Country. Our credit has become strengthened, our reputation for wealth heightened, and our importance in the family of Colonies, if not of Nations, advanced in a degree that may well make us proud and gratified as a people, scarcely emerged from the infant stages of national growth and advancement.

Peering a little into the future, we may reasonably assure ourselves that whenever the time arrives for our having recourse to borrowing, to reimburse our Consolidated Revenue Fund the sums advanced for the completion of our Railways, if their returns maintain the high standard they have now reached —an anticipation we are justified in relying upon— we shall not seek to pledge our credit for some speculative or uncertain undertaking; but we shall ask to be entrusted with moneys to pay wholly or partially, as the case may be, for the construction of a completed reproductive work, yielding a net profit almost equal to, if not exceeding, the rate of interest payable on the loan we may be seeking. This is a position of stability to be envied indeed, a position but rarely if ever attained by any Colony or Nation, and one which, from a financial point of view alone, may in all justice entitle us to the designation of the "Mother of the Australias." And let it be observed that the surplus, or in other words the proceeds of these Land Sales, whilst employed with incalculable advantage in these directions, are also at the same time assisting in opening up and improving our great national territory.

Adverting again to the large special deposits made with the Sydney Banks, I should like to make reference to, and comment upon, the observations that have been made from time to time, questioning the soundness of the policy that sanctioned these transactions. As to whether it was wise to part with such enormous areas of the public domain, as resulted in the realization of the princely surplus from which these deposits were partially and to the greatest extent made, I have now nothing to do, but will confine my remarks to the position of a Government which finds itself the trustees of an immense sum of money not needed for the current Governmental outlay. I am convinced in my own mind that the distribution of this large sum of £1,925,000 under these circumstances amongst the Banking Institutions of the city was wise and prudent; and to draw a parallel which is certainly strong, though it may not be thought quite complete, was exactly what a private individual, careful of his own interest and welfare, would have made with his own moneys, and surely a multiplicity of debtors with a division of risk is preferable to their unification.

But some persons have raised the objection that the money having been deposited in the Banks was lent by them to the pastoral tenants of the Crown to enable them to purchase and monopolize large areas of the public estate. Well, assuming, for the sake of argument, that the money was so lent, I take it that it would have been impossible for the Government, in placing this cash on deposit at interest, to impose upon the receiving Banks any conditions as to their use of it. Having reliance on the institutions in which the money was placed, and being satisfied as to their stability, the duty of the Government, so far as the Banks were concerned, was in my judgment completed.

To have prohibited any particular use of the deposits by the Banks would in all probability have resulted in their refusal to accept them, and the Government Bank—the Bank of New South Wales —would have had in that case exclusive charge of these enormous sums. Without for one single moment reflecting upon the soundness and thorough reliability of this institution, I think few persons, if any, will say that it would have been more dis-' creet or better in the general interest of the public to have confined the disposal of the Government funds to it alone; and it certainly strikes me that to have kept this immense sum in the Treasury, or to have insisted upon its being kept unemployed in the Bank's strong room, at the Treasurer's call, which would have been tantamount to the withdrawal of so much capital from circulation, would have been an act of folly of which no Treasurer at least would care of his own motion to take the responsibility. The injurious effect of such an arrangement upon the commercial and monetary interests of the Country I am sure could not be foretold. And yet it appears to me that this was the only alternative course open ; pending however the future permanent appropriation by Parliament of the surplus we are making advantageous use of it, by allowing it to fructify in the manner described.

Although the sum of £1,600,000 has been advanced from this surplus to Loan Accounts, and the greater part spent on Railway construction, I do not propose asking Parliament to interfere with the Acts authorizing the Loans to which the advances have been made; thinking it better to allow matters in this respect to remain *in statu quo*, so that the Acts may be put into operation when the necessity arises.

A very important matter in connection with our finances is the consolidation of our Public Debt, and making our securities uniform ; and the Government propose giving their earnest consideration as early as practicable to a scheme for effecting these objects, which may not alone prove of substantial pecuniary advantage, but would in all probability improve our position as a borrowing community.

As to the " Loans Accounts," I deem it unnecessary to do more than refer Honorable Members to the Statements accompanying the Ways and Means and Explanatory Statements for information concerning them.

I have now, Mr. Garrett, approached the conclusion of the important duty imposed upon me by my official position, having striven to place clearly before the Committee the exact financial status and prospects of the Country, and I tender them my warmest thanks for having so patiently borne with me.

The disastrous drought which still lingers in our midst and fills the mind with anxiety has converted large areas of our finest pasture lands into barren wastes and decimated our flocks and herds in untold numbers; but I trust that the "windows of heaven" may soon be opened, and the parched earth be once more blessed with an abundance of genial rain, so that her now sterile surface may be again enriched with the grasses, and her dried-up rivers and brooks be filled with the waters which give sustenance and life to the stock now tortured with the agonies of thirst and starvation; and painfully sensible as we may be, and no doubt are, of the seriousness of this visitation, we should not despair of the future, for a retrospect of the past must generate hope and courage.

We have a territory happily blessed with a variety of resources unsurpassed if not unequalled by those of any other country. Our progress has been such as to excite the wonder and admiration of all nations

who obtain a true and impartial knowledge of
our affairs; and with this enlightenment diffused
amongst them, from picturing us as a small and
insignificant community they begin to regard us as
an enterprising, advancing, and important Colony.
Living under the powerful sceptre of a Sovereign
whose imperial splendour radiates towards and shines
upon us, we at the same time, by the position we
are assuming as the chief of the Australian group,
contribute our small share of lustre and importance.
to the British throne.

Connected with the great centres of civilization
by an electric belt, which was erewhile looked upon
by us as the hopeless realization of a wild and
chaotic dream, we now esteem its possession as a
necessity. Fleets of magnificent steamers now vie
with each other in their efforts to secure our trade,
and are converting the once uncertain and protracted
voyage between here and Europe into a pleasure
excursion, the length of which can be reckoned to a
nicety. The merchants of all parts of the world are
competing for New South Wales commerce which
has, with giant strides, at length reached almost
incredible dimensions. Our sheep, horses, and cattle,
reduced as they have been by famine, are still num-
bered by millions, and in quality of breeding take
their places with the finest strains in Europe. Our
wool has become a most important staple in the
great manufactories of the Globe. We possess a soil
which "if you tickle it with a hoe it laughs with a

harvest." The mineral wealth we obtain from the earth, from its variety and richness, seems to vie in splendour with the star-fretted heavens that o'er-canopy us. It has influenced, and still influences, in no inconsiderable degree the money and metal markets of the world.

We have called science to our aid, and have cheerfully expended millions of pounds in piercing with the locomotive engine the mountain ranges, which with their heavy frown seemed to effectually defy the encroachments of man, and to forbid communication between the coast—the first scene of settlement in the Country—and the almost illimitable territory now covered with our flocks and herds. And these are our advantages, and the momentous interests with which we have to deal, whilst yet in the earliest stages of national existence. Determined sincerely to devote ourselves to the public business of the State, our earnestness should be co-ordinate with our responsibilities. With a high and patriotic sense of duty pervading the Parliament, and with wisdom and prudence guiding its counsels, our young Colony so beneficently favoured by a benign Providence must become great, and its people gradually mature into a contented, prosperous, and influential Nation.

D

CONSOLIDATED REVENUE FUND.

ACCOUNTS CURRENT

FOR THE YEARS

1876, 1877, AND 1878.

N(

CONSOLIDATEI

Dr. ACCOUNT of Revenue an

No.	Particulars.	Amount.	Total.
		£ s. d.	£ s. d
1	To Charges on the Consolidated Revenue Fund, as shown on page 1 of the Estimates-in-Chief for 1877, ordered to be printed 2 May, 1877 :—		
	General Services, as per Appropriation Act 40 Vic. No. 11..	3,452,453 6 3	
	Provided by Constitutional and Colonial Acts..	50,440 18 2	
	Special Appropriations	796,000 0 0	
			4,298,894 4
2	„ Additional Special Appropriations :—		
	Revenue and Receipts returned, further sum..	125,493 7 11	
	Charges on Collections, further sum	814 17 6	
	Preliminary Expenses of Municipal Institutions	216 12 10	
	Expenses of the Returning Officers of the several Electoral Districts of the Colony	370 1 5	
	Expenses under the Registration of Brands Act	351 11 3	
	Expenses under the Scab in Sheep Act of 1866	475 7 4	
	Schedule B—Superannuation, further sum	182 9 5	
			127,904 7
3	„ Amount of Debentures issued under various Acts of Parliament, paid off in 1876	....	735,800 0
4	„ Amount appropriated in aid of the Funds of the Municipal Council of Sydney, by the Act 41 Vic., No. 2, in lieu of vote of like amount for 1876, written off'	....	10,000 0
5	„ Amount of Supplementary Appropriations for Services of 1876, as per Appropriation Act, 41 Vic. No. 8..	....	102,387 7 :
	Total authorized Appropriations	....	5,274,985 19 :
6	„ Amount of Further Supplementary Estimates for Services of 1876, page 4	....	10,543 19
			5,285,529 10
7	*Less*—Amount of unused Appropriations for Services of 1876, inclusive of Appropriations for Public Works to the amount of £420,424 16s. 8d., which were re-voted as Services of 1877, written off under the provisions of the Audit Act of 1870, as per Statement attached, marked B, page 23..	....	692,716 1
	Total Estimated Expenditure for 1876	.... £	4,592,813 17 :
8	„ Estimated Accumulated Surplus at the close of 1876	....	2,096,321 19
	TOTAL ..	.... £	6,689,135 17

The Treasury, New South Wales, Sydney, 31st January, 1878.

JAMES PEARSON, Accountant.

'ENUE FUND.

ـnditure for the Year 1876.   *Cr.*

Particulars.	Amount.	Total.
	£ s. d.	£ s. d.
By Estimated Surplus on the Account for the Year 1875, as shown in Accounts Nos. 1 and 2 of the Ways and Means of 1877, which were ordered to be printed, 2ud May, 1877	1,615,525 17 3	
Add—Difference between the Actual Surplus on the Account for the Year 1875, and the Estimated Surplus, as above shown, thus :— Actual Surplus as now ascertained ., .. £1,655,307 10 9 Estimated Surplus, as shown above .. 1,615,525 17 3	39,781 13 6	1,655,307 10 9
,, Actual Revenue for the Year 1876, as per Statement attached, marked A, page 17	5,037,661 16 6	
Less—Repayments of Advances credited to Votes..	3,833 10 3	5,033,828 6 3
TOTAL	....	£ 6,689,135 17 0

JAMES THOMSON,
    Consulting Accountant.

H. E. COHEN,
    Treasurer,

Nc

CONSOLIDATEI

ACCOUNT of Revenue an

Dr.

No.	Particulars.	Amount.	Total.	
		£ s. d.	£ s. d.	
	To Charges on the Consolidated Revenue Fund, as per Estimates-in-Chief for 1878, page 1 :—			
	General Services (as per Appropriation Act, 41 Vic. No. 8)	4,096,248 15 2		
	Provided by Constitutional and Colonial Acts	47,946 16 8		
	Special Appropriations	837,000 0 0		
			5,581,195 11 1	
2	,, Additional Special Appropriations :—			
	Revenue and Receipts returned, further sum	141,754 16 8		
	Charges on Collections, further sum	1,226 4 4		
	Preliminary Expenses of Municipal Institutions..	119 15 4		
	Expenses of the Returning Officers of the several Electoral Districts of the Colony.. .. .. '.	6,463 15 6		
	Debentures paid off	7,800 0 0		
	Expenses under the Scab in Sheep and Imported Stock Acts.. ..	1,009 9 3		
	Premium on Debentures purchased in accordance with Acts 31 Victoria No. 11, and 36 Victoria No. 2	279 17 6		
			159,253 18	
	Total authorized Charges ..	....	5,740,449 10	
3	,, Amount of Supplementary Estimates for Services of 1877, page 9 ..	....	100,407 7	
			5,840,856 17 1	
4	*Less*—Amount of Appropriations for Services of 1877, estimated as not likely to be required	250,000 0 0		
	and			
	Amount of Vote taken to enable the Treasurer to make Advances to Public Officers and others, &c., during 1877, which will not ultimately form a charge on the Consolidated Revenue Fund	60,000 0 0		
			310,000 0	
	Total Estimated Expenditure for 1877	....	5,530,856 17 1	
5	,, Estimated Accumulated Surplus, 31st December, 1877	....	2,317,343 10 1	
	TOTAL .. .. :..	....	£ 7,848,200 8	

The Treasury, New South Wales,
Sydney, 31st January, 1878.

JAMES PEARSON,
Accountant.

REVENUE FUND.

Expenditure for the Year 1877.

Cr.

No.	Particulars.	Amount.	Total.
		£ s. d.	£ s. d.
1	By Estimated Accumulated Surplus at the close of 1876, brought forward	....	2,096,321 19 2
2	„ Amount of Actual Revenue for the Year 1877, as per Statement attached, marked A, page 17	....	5,751,878 9 6
	TOTAL .. .. £	....	7,848,200 8

JAMES THOMSON,
Consulting Accountant.

H. E. COHEN,
Treasurer.

No.

CONSOLIDATED

Dr. ACCOUNT of Estimated Revenue and

Particulars.	Amount.	Total.
	£ s. d.	£ s. d.
To Charges on the Consolidated Revenue Fund, as per Estimates-in-Chief for 1878, page 1 :—		
General Services	3,909,556 0 0	
Provided by Constitutional and Colonial Acts	47,133 4 2	
Special Appropriations	797,000 0 0	
		4,753,689 4 2
Less—Amount of Vote to enable the Treasurer to make Advances to Public Officers and others, &c., during 1878, which will not ultimately form a charge on the Consolidated Revenue Fund	....	30,000 0 0
Total Estimated Expenditure for 1878 .. £	....	4,723,689 4 2
,, Estimated Accumulated Surplus, 31st December, 1878	....	2,467,404 6 8
Total .. .. .. £	....	7,191,093 10 10

Treasury, New South Wales,
 Sydney, 31st January, 1878.

JAMES PEARSON,
Accountant.

3.

REVENUE FUND.

Expenditure for the Year 1878.   *Cr.*

No.	Particulars.	Amount.	Total.
		£ s. d.	£ s. d.
1	By Estimated Surplus on the Account for the year 1877, brought forward	....	2,317,343 10 0
2	„ Estimated Revenue for the Year 1878, as per Statement attached, marked A, page 17	....	4,873,750 0 0
	TOTAL	....	£ 7,191,093 10 10

JAMES THOMSON,
  Consulting Accountant.

H. E. COHEN,
  Treasurer.

5858

A.
CONSOLIDATED REVENUE.

ABSTRACT Statement showing the Actual Revenue of the Years 1876 and 1877, and the Estimated Revenue for the year 1878.

Head of Receipt.	Revenue of 1876.	Revenue of 1877.	Estimated Revenue for 1878.
Taxation.	£	£	£
Customs	1,011,872	1,074,733	1,094,700
Duty on Refined Sugar and Molasses	35,975	39,867	40,000
Duty on Spirits distilled in the Colony	9,860	8,169	8,000
Stamps	455	1,657	....
Duty on Gold	9,368	7,458	7,500
Licenses	93,876	101,249	102,500
Total Taxation	1,161,406	1,233,133	1,252,700
Land Revenue.			
SALES	2,414,075	2,841,203	1,855,000
ANNUAL LAND REVENUE—			
Interest on Land conditionally purchased	99,329	126,654	155,000
Pastoral Occupation	222,092	230,106	237,450
Mining Occupation	13,214	11,211	13,000
Miscellaneous Land Receipts	24,293	27,163	28,500
	358,928	395,134	433,950
Total Land Revenue	2,773,003	3,236,337	2,288,950
Receipts for Services rendered.			
Railway Receipts	678,392	799,897	875,000
Post Office	190,882	224,449	229,500
Mint Receipts	10,496	10,903	10,500
Fees for Escort and Conveyance of Gold	2,640	1,890	2,000
Pilotage, Harbour, and Light Rates and Fees	27,333	28,795	30,000
Registration of Brands	1,188	844	800
Contributions under Sheep Diseases Prevention Act of 1866	11,029	10.233	10,000
Fees of Office	43,368	42,348	45,600
Total Receipts for Services rendered	965,328	1,119,359	1,203,400
General Miscellaneous Receipts.			
Rents, exclusive of Land	31,070	24,069	7,000
Fines and Forfeitures	8,635	8,988	9,550
Unclassified Receipts	98,220	129,993	112,150
Total Miscellaneous Receipts	137,925	163,050	128,700
Grand Totals £	5,037,662	5,751,879	4,873,750

The Treasury, New South Wales, Sydney, 31st January, 1878.

H. E. COHEN, Treasurer.

REVENUE DETAILED.

Head of Receipt.	Revenue of 1876.	Revenue of 1877.	Estimated Revenue for 1878.
Taxation.	£	£	£
CUSTOMS.			
Spirits	442,869	476,870	· 480,000
Wine	36,146	37,521	40,000
Ale and Beer ... ...· ...	35,196	33,467·	35,000
Tobacco and Cigars	75,230	94,798	95,000
Tea	60,494	63,004	65,000
Sugar and Molasses... · '... ...	40,529	47,486	50,000
Coffee and Chicory	7,979	8,918	10,000
Opium	8,350·	8,362	10,000
Malt	4,395	5,599	7,000
Hops	6,134	5,699	7,000
Rice	9,748	9,430	10,000
Dried Fruits	31,702	40,187	40,000
Specific Duties	127,944	155,726	160,000
Bonded Warehouses, 20 Vic. No. 21 ...	4,895	5,484	5,500
Rent of Goods in Queen's Warehouses, &c.	200	140	200
	891,811	992,691	1,014,700
Murray River Customs	120,061	82,042	80,000
	1,011,872	1,074,733	1,094,700
DUTY ON REFINED SUGAR AND MOLASSES ...	35,975	39,867	40,000
DUTY ON SPIRITS DISTILLED IN THE COLONY	9,860	8,169	8,000
STAMPS	455	1,657	....
DUTY ON GOLD	9,368	7,458	7,500
LICENSES.			
Wholesale Spirit Dealers	4,380	4,990	5,000
Auctioneers	2,250	2,272	· 2,400
Retail Fermented and Spirituous Liquors...	80,302	86,602	87,500
Billiard and Bagatelle Licenses	4,095	4,155	4,000
Distillers and Rectifiers	83	74	100
Hawkers and Pedlers	1,215	1,367	1,500
Pawnbrokers...	600	570	600
Colonial Wine, Cider, and Perry Licenses...	448	519	600
Licenses under the Gunpowder Act of 1876	205	314	400
All other Licenses	298	386	400
	93,876	101,249	102,500
TOTAL TAXATION... ... £	1,161,406	1,233,133	1,252,700

	1876.	1877.
NOTE.—To the Murray River Customs for 1876 and 1877 as above shown, viz. :—	£120,061	82,042
There should be added the amounts collected at the undermentioned Bonds (which were established towards the close of the former year) included under the general Customs, viz. :—		
Deniliquin	4,042	24,319
Hay	302	7,573
Wilcannia	1,833	5,667
Total actual collections	£126,928	119,601
To which has also to be added the amount due by the Government of South Australia on the 31st December last .. ·.	....	11,368
	£126,928	130,969

REVENUE DETAILED—*continued.*

Head of Receipt.	Revenue of 1876.	Revenue of 1877.	Estimated Revenue for 1878.
Land Revenue.	£	£	£
SALES.			
Auction Sales	1,469,648	1,967,057	1,000,000
Improved Purchases, &c.	91,596	133,358	200,000
Selections after Auction	98,280	166,730	160,000
Provisional Pre-emptive Right Sales	189,664	77,263	....
Deposits on Conditional Purchases	496,053	424,954	425,000
Instalments on Conditional Purchases	7,134	10,751	10,000
Balances on Conditional Purchases	61,700	61,090	60,000
TOTAL REVENUE FROM LAND SALES ...£	2,414,075	2,841,203	1,855,000
Annual Land Revenue.			
INTEREST ON LAND CONDITIONALLY PURCHASED	99,329	126,654	155,000
PASTORAL OCCUPATION.			
Rent of Annual Leases	48,871	51,176	65,000
Rent of Runs	172,088	176,305	170,000
Assessment on Runs	938	2,376	2,200
Quit Rents	195	249	250
	222,092	230,106	237,450
MINING OCCUPATION.			
Mineral Leases	7,178	5,563	7,000
Mineral Licenses	251	390	500
Leases of Auriferous Lands	1,936	2,001	2,000
Miners' Rights	3,370	2,807	3,000
Business Licenses	479	450	500
	13,214	11,211	13,000
MISCELLANEOUS LAND RECEIPTS.			
Licenses to cut Timber, &c.	4,256	4,330	4,300
Fees on Transfer of Runs	1,308	1,232	1,200
Fees on Preparation and Enrolment of Title Deeds	12,185	14,369	15,000
All other Receipts	6,544	7,232	8,000
	24,293	27,163	28,500
TOTAL ANNUAL LAND REVENUE ......£	358,928	395,134	433,950

REVENUE DETAILED—*continued.*

Head of Receipt.	Revenue of 1876.	Revenue of 1877.	Estimated Revenue for 1878.
Receipts for Services rendered.	£	£	£
RAILWAY RECEIPTS	678,392	799,897	875,000
POST OFFICE.			
Postage	126,802	151,959	154,000
Telegraph Receipts	59,417	67,298	70,000
Commission on Money Orders	4,663	5,192	5,500
	190,882	224,449	229,500
MINT RECEIPTS	10,496	10,903	10,500
FEES FOR ESCORT AND CONVEYANCE OF GOLD	2,640	1,890	2,000
PILOTAGE, HARBOUR, AND LIGHT RATES AND FEES	27,333	28,795	30,000
REGISTRATION OF BRANDS	1,188	844	800
CONTRIBUTIONS UNDER THE SHEEP DISEASE PREVENTION ACT OF 1866	11,029	10,233	10,000
FEES OF OFFICE.			
Certificates of Naturalization	131	146	150
Registrar General	10,989	12,530	14,000
Prothonotary of Supreme Court	3,099	3,336	3,500
Master in Equity	696	466	550
Curator of Intestate Estates	374	799	700
Insolvent Court	1,739	1,760	1,800
Sheriff	729	702	750
District Courts	4,672	4,890	5,000
Courts of Petty Sessions	4,848	4,156	6,000
Shipping Masters	2,646	2,765	3,000
Slaughtering Fees, Globe Island Abattoir	1,832	1,956	2,150
Other Fees	11,613	8,842	8,000
	43,368	42,348	45,600
TOTAL RECEIPTS FOR SERVICES RENDERED £	965,328	1,119,359	1,203,400

REVENUE DETAILED—*continued*.

Head of Receipt.	Revenue of 1876.	Revenue of 1877.	Estimated Revenue for 1878.
General Miscellaneous Receipts.			
RENTS, EXCLUSIVE OF LAND.	£	£.	£
Tolls and Ferries	22,762	17,802	....
Wharfs ... ... \	5,788	3,698	5,000
Government Buildings and Premises ...	54	3	50
Glebe Island Bridge	985	750	....
Glebe Island Abattoir	1,481	1,816	1,950
	31,070	24,069	7,000
FINES AND FORFEITURES.			
Sheriff	561	167	600
Courts of Petty Sessions	7,416	7,951	8,000
Unauthorized Occupation of Crown Lands	205	392	450
Crown's Share of Seizures, &c.	130	202	150
Confiscated and Unclaimed Property ...	250	258	300
Other Fines	73	18	50
	8,635	8,988	9,550
UNCLASSIFIED RECEIPTS.			
Sale of Government Property	1,840	2,373	2,500
Support of Patients in Lunatic Asylums ...	1,652	1,644	1,500
Collections by Government Printer ...	4,447.	4,418	4,500
Store Rent of Gunpowder	617	1,727	1,400
Work performed by Prisoners in Gaol ...	3,207	3,440	3,750
Fees on presenting Private Bills to Parliament and on Letters of Registration...	1,400	1,595	1,000
Interest on Bank Deposits...	52,629	89,130	75,000
Fitz Roy Dry Dock Receipts	2,892	1,423	1,500
Assessment on Sugar Refinery	1,000	750	1,000
Other Receipts	28,536	23,493	20,000
	98,220	129,993	112,150
Total, General Miscellaneous Receipts... £	137,925	163,050	128,700
Grand Totals .. .. £	5,037,662	5,751,879	4,873,750

The Treasury, New South Wales,   · H. E. COHEN,
    Sydney, 31st January, 1878.   Treasurer.

STATEMENT OF THE BALANCES

ON THE

PUBLIC ACCOUNTS OF NEW SOUTH WALES,

AND THE DISTRIBUTION OF THE SAME

ON THE

31st DECEMBER, 1877.

STATEMENT of Balances on the Public Accounts of New South Wales,

TREASURY BALANCES. Public Account.	£ s. d.	£ s.
Consolidated Revenue— Revenue Proper	....	*2,351,073 15
Loans' Account (Old)	....	178,915 2 1
Trust Fund—		
Church and School Estates Fund	173,445 14 9	
Superannuation Fund, 27 Vict. No. 11	384 1 6	
Police Reward Fund	7,598 17 6	
Police Superannuation Fund	13,776 11 5	
Poundage	12,876 8 6	
Shipping Master (Seamen's Wages)	688 3 0	
Revenue Suspense Fund	27,254 16 10	
Trust Moneys, 20 Vict. No. 11	68,037 8 8	
Immigration Remittances	17,699 7 10	
Commissioners' Fund—Real Property Act	703 5 0	
Assurance Fund—Real Property Act	21,675 7 9	
Government Savings Bank Account, 34 Vict. No. 15	466,222 14 4	
Money Order Account	96 19 1	
British and Australian Telegraph Account	5,711 2 2	
Railway Store Account	7,876 18 0	
Imperial Pension Fund Commission Account	102 10 6	
Over-issues	35,737 18 4	
Treasurer's Advance Account	20,509 18 11	
Gold Fields Survey Fee Account	1,562 14 6	
Advances to Contractors Account	1,249 18 9	
San Francisco Mail Service Account	7,499 16 5	
New Zealand Cable Account	591 11 5	
Sundry Deposits	115,123 3 6	1,006,425 8
Total Public Account	....	3,536,414 7
Loan Funds.		
The Loan Fund, 35 Vic. No. 5	5,143 0 1	
The Loan Fund, 36 Vic. No. 2	9,866 5 4	
The Loan Fund Funded Stock Act of 1873, 36 Vic. No. 21	145,970 16 8	
The Loan Fund Railway Loan Act, 36 Vic. No. 17	108,257 16 7	
The Superannuation Repeal Fund, 36 Vic. No. 20	3,757 13 5	
The Loan Fund, 38 Vic. No. 2	25,886 1 4	
The Loan Fund, 39 Vic. No. 18	18,784 12 6	
The Loan Fund, 40 Vic. No. 12	32,546 5 11	
The Loan Fund, 41 Vic. No. 4	88,387 13 5	
The Loan Fund, 41 Vic. No. 7	96,132 18 0	534,733 3
TOTAL		£ 4,071,147 10

* In addition to this balance there is a sum of £1,600,000 to be recovered from Loan Funds,

The Treasury New South Wales,
11th January, 1878.

and the distribution of the same on the 31st December, 1877.

DISTRIBUTION OF THE BALANCES.		£ s. d.	£ s. d.
Bank of New South Wales—			
London Account—			
Balance as per account of 31st August, 1877, the date of latest advices received in time for passing through the books of the Treasury £16,125 9 1			
Amount of remittances prior to that date, not included therein 650,000 0 0			
Amount of Remittances since that date.. .. .. 100,000 0 0			766,125 9 1
Public Account, Sydney 380,032 8 4			
Less—Unpresented Cheques 14,126 9 9			365,005 18 7
Loan Funds :—			
The Loan Fund, 35 Vic. No. 5		5,143 0 1	
The Loan Fund, 36 Vic. No. 2		9,866 5 4	
The Loan Fund, 36 Vic. No. 17		108,257 16 7	
The Loan Fund Funded Stock Act of 1873, 36 Vic. No. 21		20,970 16 8	
The Superannuation Repeal Fund, 36 Vic. No. 20		3,757 13 5	
The Loan Fund, 38 Vic. No. 2		25,886 1 4	
The Loan Fund, 39 Vic. No. 18..		18,784 12 6	
The Loan Fund, 40 Vic. No. 12..		32,546 5 11	
The Loan Fund, 41 Vic. No. 4		88,387 13 5	
The Loan Fund, 41 Vic. No. 7		96,132 18 0	1,541,764 10 11
Special Deposits :—			
Bank of New South Wales		350,000 0 0	
Australian Joint Stock Bank		200,000 0 0	
City Bank		250,000 0 0	
Oriental Bank		250,000 0 0	
Bank of Australasia		175,000 0 0	
Union Bank of Australia..		175,000 0 0	
English, Scottish, and Australian Chartered Bank..		175,000 0 0	
London Chartered Bank		175,000 0 0	
Mercantile Bank		175,000 0 0	1,925,000 0 0
Cash in hands of the Receiver (subsequently banked).. ..		....	28,770 18 8
Securities in the Treasury Chest, viz. :—			
Police Reward and Superannuation Fund—Debentures		10,200 0 0	
Church and School Estates Revenue Fund—			
Debentures £46,400 0 0			
New South Wales Four per Cents 106,781 19 3		153,181 19 3	
Assurance Fund—Debentures		16,300 0 0	
Government Savings Bank—			
Debentures £89,200 0 0			
New South Wales Four per Cents 291,675 1 4		380,875 1 4	
Other Securities		6,055 0 4	575,612 0 11
TOTAL			£ 4,071,147 10 6

being the amount of advances from the Consolidated Revenue Fund pending the sale of Debentures.

JAMES PEARSON,
Accountant

E

www.ingramcontent.com/pod-product-compliance
Lightning Source LLC
Chambersburg PA
CBHW021525090426
42739CB00007B/789

* 9 7 8 3 3 3 7 1 5 1 3 1 7 *